I0087452

Gustav
HOLST

Second Suite in F
Op. 28 No. 2

(Richard W. Sargeant, Jr.)

Study Score
Partitur

SERENISSIMA MUSIC, INC.

Holst composed the "Second Suite" in 1911, employing seven different English folk songs as the primary melodic material. Three of the tunes are found in the first movement alone. First the morris-dance "Glorishears" (bar 3), then "Swansea Town" (bar 47), and finally "Claudy Banks" (used the for Trio at bar 111). The second movement is based upon the Cornish folksong "I'll Love My Love", while the third quotes "A Blacksmith Courted Me". The Finale uses "Dargason" throughout with "Greensleeves" appearing at measures 57 and again at 145. While these two might not be actual folk songs they were taken from John Playford's well-known collection of 16th and 17th Century dance tunes. As with the First Suite, the specific occasion and ensemble for which this work was written remains obscure.

In contrast to its predecessor which featured elastic scoring, Holst was quite specific about the instrumental forces required for the "Second Suite." In 1948 Boosey & Hawkes issued a revised set with a full score which added many instruments that Holst never intended. The additional instruments are alto clarinet, bass clarinet, contrabass clarinet, soprano saxophone, baritone saxophone, bass saxophone and 2 B-flat trumpets. For the present edition all added instruments except the bass clarinet and baritone saxophone have been eliminated. These two added parts, generally considered necessary in most bands and wind ensembles, are based upon the original Boosey issue. The serious misprint in measures 19-22 of the 3rd movement in the bass clarinet, which should double the bassoons and tenor saxophone, has been corrected. The baritone saxophone, which doubles tuba much of the time in the Boosey part, has been omitted in the places where there is only brass playing and from the second movement altogether.

One important issue in the manuscript score concerns Holst's intentions for the opening solo in the second movement. The manuscript while somewhat confusing clearly states 'Melody for oboe or clar.' However, the melody itself is written only in the solo Clarinet line while the Oboe has accompaniment material. The most logical interpretation is that Holst wished for the solo to be taken by the Oboe - using a solo clarinet only if no oboe was available. The only difference from the manuscript in the present edition is the inclusion of both the solo melody and the accompaniment material in the oboe part. For the accompaniment, Holst clearly wrote 'one player only' in the clarinet staves and surely did not expect to have doubling in any of the other woodwind parts, who should play one on a part until measure 18. The brass should be one player on a part throughout the movement with the exception of the tuba - which should have two players from 19 through 31. The numerous errors found in the 1948 score have been corrected without comment, along with minor changes to keep articulations and phrasing consistent.

Richard W. Sargeant, Jr.
December, 2011

Holst's Original Instrumentation

Flute / Piccolo in D-flat
Oboe
Solo and 1st Clarinet in B-flat
2nd Clarinet in B-flat
3rd Clarinet in B-flat
[Alto] Saxophone in E-flat
[Tenor] Saxophone in B-flat
2 Bassoons

Solo and 1st Cornet in B-flat
2nd Cornet in B-flat
4 Horns in E-flat and F
2 Tenor Trombones
Bass Trombone
Euphonium
Basses

Percussion
(Side Drum, Triangle, Bass Drum, Cymbals, Tambourine, Anvil)

Duration: ca. 11 minutes

First documented performace: June 22, 1922
London: Royal Albert Hall
Royal Military School of Music Band
Col. J.A.C. Somerville, conductor

ISBN: 978-160874-052-9
Printed in the USA
First Printing: December, 2011

SECOND SUITE FOR MILITARY BAND
in F

1. March

Gustav Holst
Edited by Richard W. Sargeant, Jr.

Copyright © Serenissima Music, Inc.
All rights reserved.   Printed in USA

12
19
Picc.
Fl. 1 2
Ob.
E♭ Cl.
Cl. 1 2 3
B. Cl.
Bn. 1 2
Alto Sax.
Ten. Sax.
Bari. Sax.
12
19
Cor. 1 2
Hn. 1 2 3 4
Trb. 1 2
Bass
Eph.
Basses
tgl.
Per.
Cymb. B. D.
p

23
27
Picc.
Fl. 1 2
Ob.
E♭ Cl.
Cl. 1 2 3
B. Cl.
Bn. 1 2
Alto Sax.
Ten. Sax.
Bari. Sax.
Cor. 1 2
Hn. 1 2 3 4
Trb. 1 2
Bass
Eph.
Basses
Per.
S. D.
Cymb. B. D.
f

35
47
Picc.
Fl. 1 2
a2
Ob.
E♭ Cl.
Cl. 1 2 3
B. Cl.
Bn. 1 2
Alto Sax.
Ten. Sax.
Bari. Sax.
Cor. 1 2
Hn. 1 2 3 4
Trb. 1 2
Bass
Eph.
(solo)
Basses
Per.
Cymb.
B. D.
f
dim.
p
mf

48
Picc.
Fl. 1 2
Ob.
E♭ Cl.
Cl. 1 2 3
B. Cl.
Bn. 1 2
Alto Sax.
Ten. Sax.
Bari. Sax.
48
Cor. 1 2
Hn. 1 2 3 4
Trb. 1 2 Bass
Eph.
Basses
Per.
Cymb.
B. D.

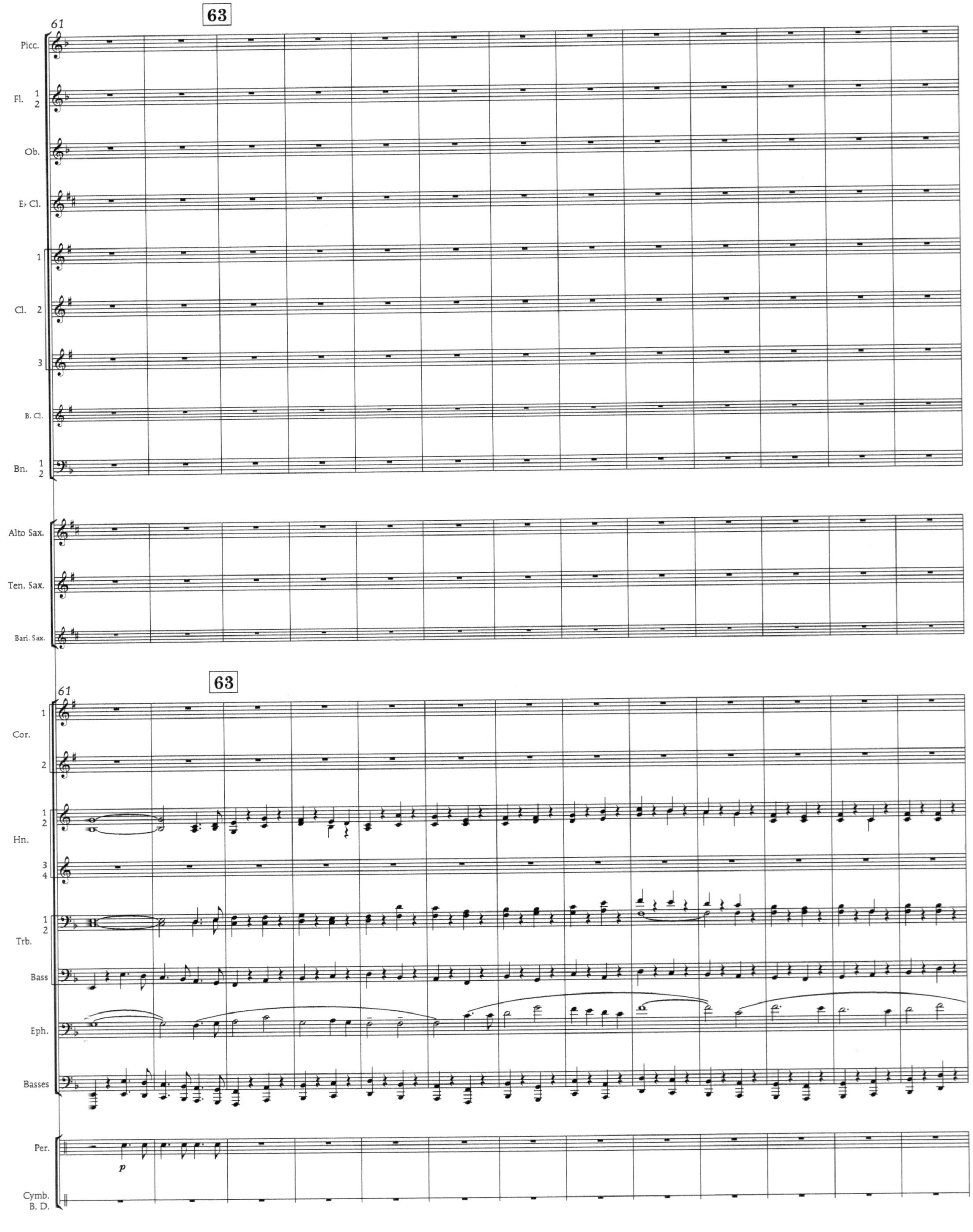
61
63
Picc.
Fl. 1 2
Ob.
E♭ Cl.
Cl. 1 2 3
B. Cl.
Bn. 1 2
Alto Sax.
Ten. Sax.
Bari. Sax.
61
63
Cor. 1 2
Hn. 1 2 3 4
Trb. 1 2
Bass
Eph.
Basses
Per.
p
Cymb.
B. D.

74
79
Picc.
Fl. 1 2
a2
Ob.
E♭ Cl.
Cl. 1 2 3
B. Cl.
Bn. 1 2
Alto Sax.
Ten. Sax.
Bari. Sax.
Cor. 1 2
Hn. 1 2 3 4
Trb. 1 2
Bass
Eph.
(tutti)
Basses
Per.
Cymb. B. D.
ff
p cresc.
cresc.

89
Picc.
Fl. 1 2
Ob.
E♭ Cl.
Cl. 1 2 3
B. Cl.
Bn. 1 2
Alto Sax.
Ten. Sax.
Bari. Sax.
89
Cor. 1 2
Hn. 1 2 3 4
Trb. 1 2 Bass
Eph.
Basses
Per.
ff
Cymb. B. D.

40529

116
Picc.
Fl. 1 2
Ob.
E♭ Cl.
Cl. 1 2 3
B. Cl.
Bn. 1 2
Alto Sax.
Ten. Sax.
Bari. Sax.
116
Cor. 1 2
Hn. 1 2 3 4
Trb. 1 2
Bass
Eph.
Basses
Per.
Cymb.
B. D.

127
128
Picc.
Fl. 1 2
a2
Ob.
E♭ Cl.
Cl. 1 2 3
B. Cl.
Bn. 1 2
Alto Sax.
Ten. Sax.
Bari. Sax.
Cor. 1 2
Hn. 1 2 3 4
Trb. 1 2
Bass
Eph.
Basses
Per.
Cymb. B. D.

14

149
152
D. C. al Fine
Picc.
Fl. 1 2
Ob.
E♭ Cl.
Cl. 1 2 3
B. Cl.
Bn. 1 2
Alto Sax.
Ten. Sax.
Bari. Sax.
ff
149
152
D. C. al Fine
Cor. 1 2
Hn. 1 2 3 4
Trb. 1 2
Bass
Eph.
Basses
Per.
Cymb. B. D.
ff

2. Song without Words
'I'll Love My Love'

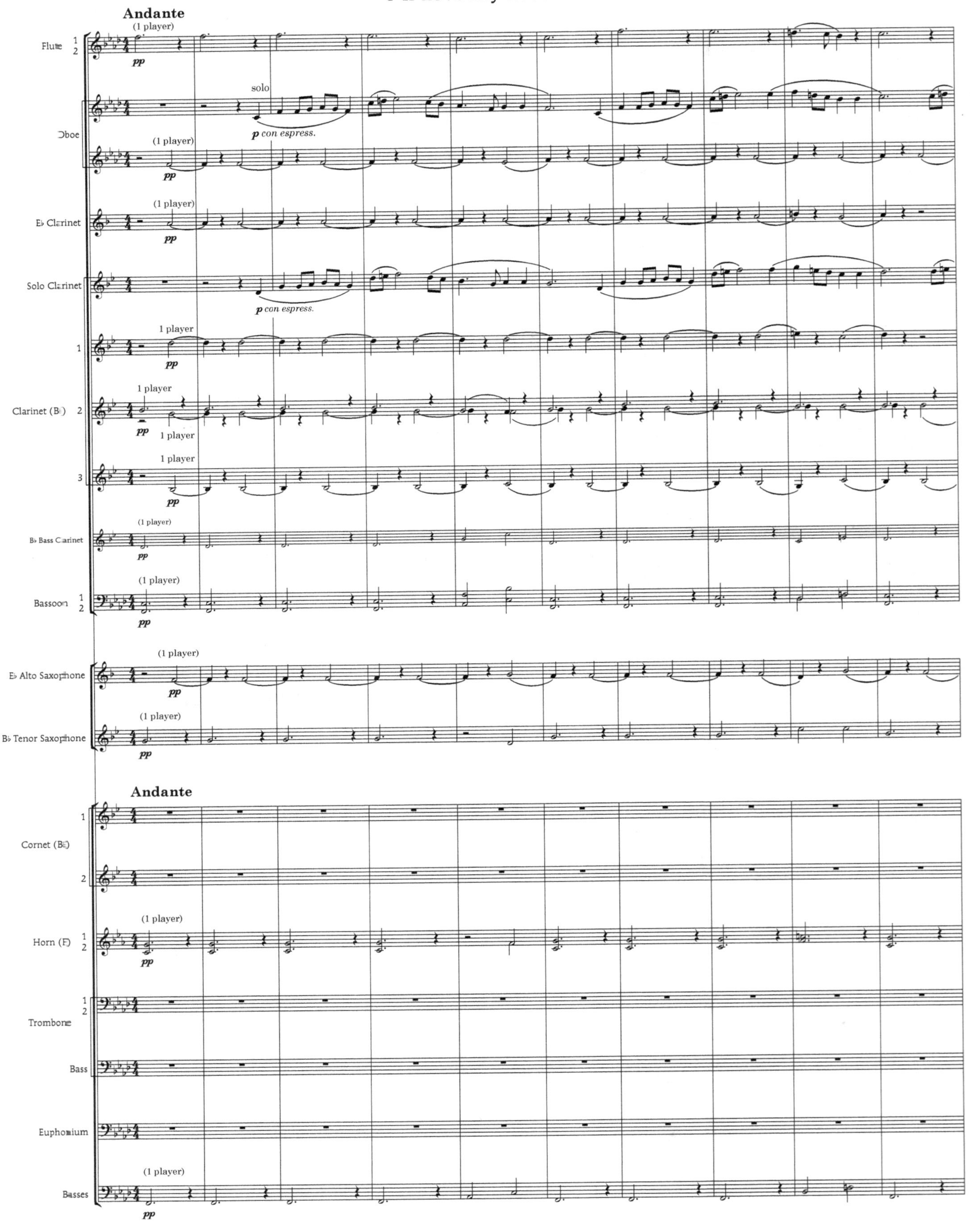

11
ad lib.
18
atempo
Fl. 1 2
a2 (tutti)
p
Ob.
(tutti)
(tutti)
E♭ Cl.
(tutti)
p
Solo Cl.
1
tutti
Cl. 2
1 player
tutti
3
tutti
B. Cl.
(tutti)
pp
Bn. 1 2
a2 (tutti)
pp
Alto Sax.
(tutti)
Ten. Sax.
(tutti)
pp
11
ad lib.
18
atempo
Cor. 1
solo
p
2
Hn. 1 2
Trb. 1 2
(1 player)
pp
Bass
(1 player)
pp
Eph.
(1 player)
pp
Basses
(2 players)

18

40529

29
ad lib.
(atempo)
Fl. 1 2
pp
Ob.
pp
E♭ Cl.
pp
solo
pp
Cl. 1 2 3
B. Cl.
Bn. 1 2
Alto Sax.
solo
pp
Ten. Sax.
pp
29
ad lib.
(atempo)
div. (2 players)
Cor. 1 2
pp
pp
a2
Hn. 1 2
Trb. 1 2
pp
Bass
pp
Eph.
pp
solo
pp
Basses
solo
pp

3. Song of the Blacksmith

8
11
Picc.
Fl. 1 2
Ob.
E♭ Cl.
Cl. 1 2 3
B. Cl.
mf
Bn. 1 2
a2
mf
Alto Sax.
Ten. Sax.
Bari. Sax.
8
11
Cor. 1 2
solo
f
Hn. 1 2 3 4
a2
a2
Trb. 1 2
Bass
Eph.
Basses
Per.
Cymb. B. D.

22

21
24
Picc.
Fl. 1 2
Ob.
E♭ Cl.
Cl. 1 2 3
B. Cl.
Bn. 1 2
Alto Sax.
Ten. Sax.
Bari. Sax.
Cor. 1 2
Hn. 1 2 3 4
Trb. 1 2
Bass
Eph.
Basses
Per.
Cymb. B. D.
div.
cresc.
p cresc.
f
fff

24

40529

4. Fantasia on the "Dargason"

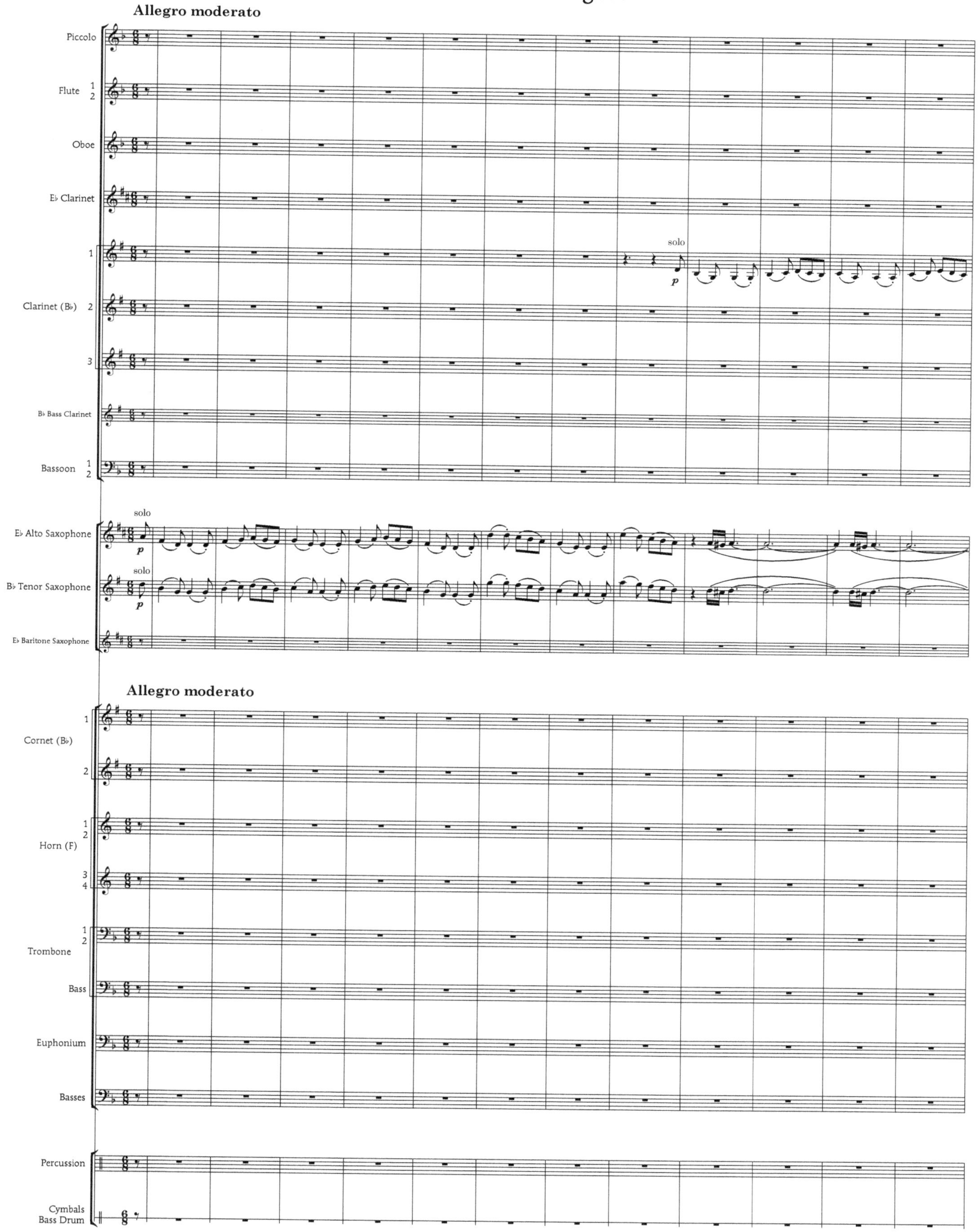

17
13
Picc.
Fl. 1 2
Ob.
E♭ Cl.
Cl. 1 2 3
tutti
p senza cresc.
B. Cl.
Bn. 1 2
Alto Sax.
(tutti)
Ten. Sax.
(tutti)
Bari. Sax.
17
13
Cor. 1 2
Hn. 1 2 3 4
pp
Trb. 1 2
Bass
Eph.
Basses
Per.
tgl.
Cymb. B. D.

24
Picc.
Fl. 1 2
Ob.
p cresc.
E♭ Cl.
p cresc.
1
cresc.
Cl. 2
cresc.
3
cresc.
B. Cl.
cresc.
Bn. 1 2
a2
cresc.
Alto Sax.
cresc.
Ten. Sax.
cresc.
Bari. Sax.
cresc.
24
Cor. 1 2
p cresc.
Hn. 1 2
cresc.
a2
p cresc.
3 4
Trb. 1 2
p cresc.
Bass
Eph.
Basses
cresc.
Per.
p cresc.
Cymb. B. D.

41
35
Picc.
Fl. 1 2
a2
Ob.
E♭ Cl.
Cl. 1 2 3
B. Cl.
Bn. 1 2
Alto Sax.
Ten. Sax.
Bari. Sax.
f
41
35
Cor. 1 2
Hn. 1 2 3 4
Trb. 1 2
a2
Bass
mf cresc.
Eph.
mf cresc.
Basses
Per.
tamb.
Cymb. B. D.

46
Picc.
Fl. 1 2
Ob.
E♭ Cl.
Cl. 1 2 3
B. Cl.
Bn. 1 2
Alto Sax.
Ten. Sax.
Bari. Sax.
Cor. 1 2
Hn. 1 2 3 4
Trb. 1 2
Bass
Eph.
Basses
Per.
Cymb. B. D.
dim.
p
pp
tgl.

30

57 (one beat in a bar but keep the same pace as before)

57 (one beat in a bar but keep the same pace as before)

40529

69
Picc.
Fl. 1 2
Ob.
E♭ Cl.
Cl. 1 2 3
B. Cl.
Bn. 1 2
Alto Sax.
Ten. Sax.
Bari. Sax.
69
Cor. 1 2
solo
p cantabile
Hn. 1 2 3 4
Trb. 1 2
Bass
Eph.
Basses
Per.
Cymb.
B. D.

89 two beats in a bar
81
Picc.
Fl. 1 2
Ob.
E♭ Cl.
Cl. 1 2 3
B. Cl.
Bn. 1 2
Alto Sax.
Ten. Sax.
Bari. Sax.
dim.
p
a2
89 two beats in a bar
81
Cor. 1 2
Hn. 1 2 3 4
Trb. 1 2
Bass
Eph.
Basses
Per.
Cymb. B. D.

93
Picc.
Fl. 1 2
Ob.
E♭ Cl.
Cl. 1 2 3
B. Cl.
Bn. 1 2
Alto Sax.
Ten. Sax.
Bari. Sax.
Cor. 1 2
(tutti)
Hn. 1 2 3 4
a2
Trb. 1 2
Bass
Eph.
Basses
Per.
Cymb. B. D.

34

40529

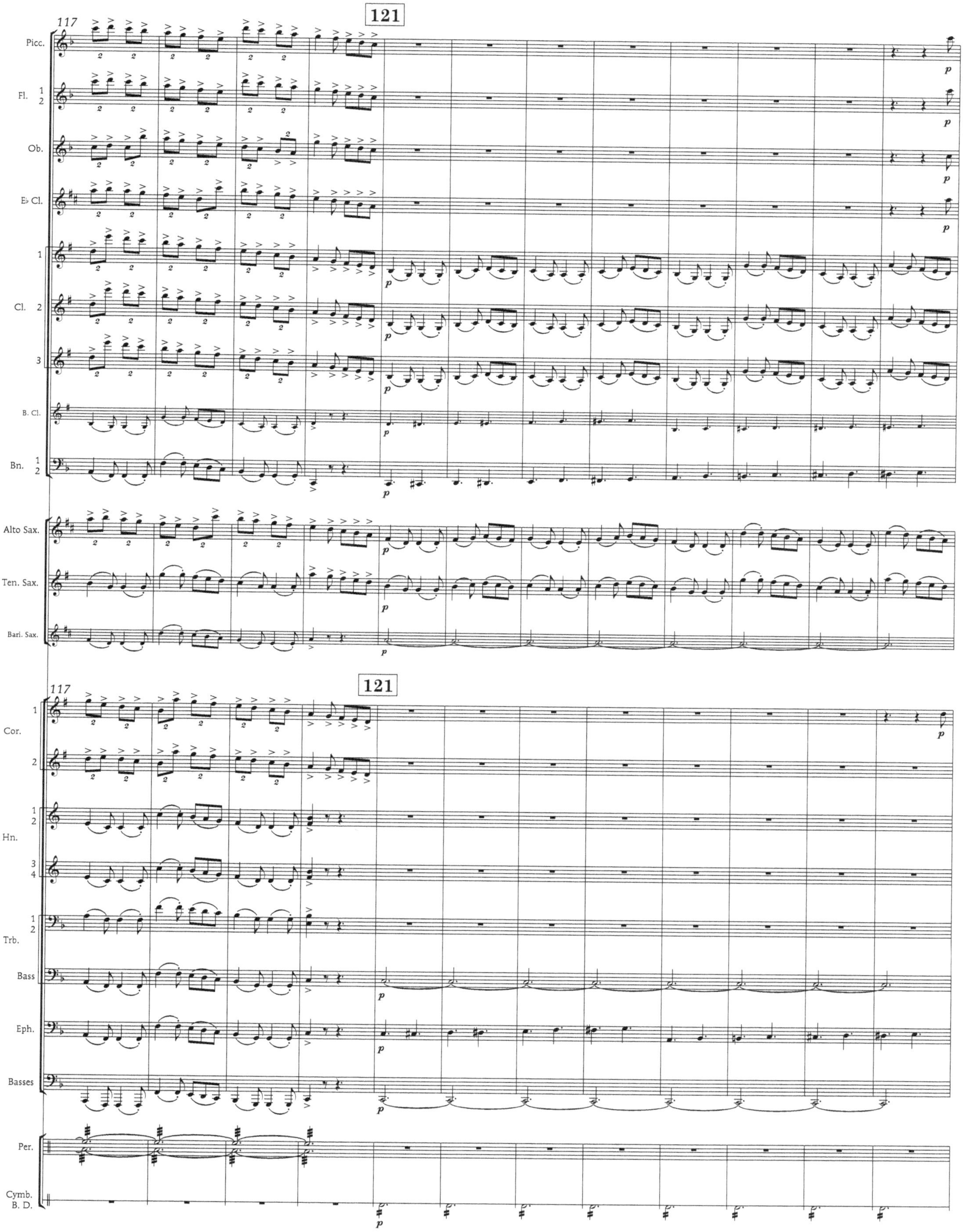
117
121
Picc.
Fl. 1 2
Ob.
E♭ Cl.
Cl. 1 2 3
B. Cl.
Bn. 1 2
Alto Sax.
Ten. Sax.
Bari. Sax.
117
121
Cor. 1 2
Hn. 1 2 3 4
Trb. 1 2 Bass
Eph.
Basses
Per.
Cymb. B. D.

129
Picc.
Fl. 1 2
Ob.
E♭ Cl.
Cl. 1 2 3
B. Cl.
Bn. 1 2
Alto Sax.
Ten. Sax.
Bari. Sax.
Cor. 1 2
Hn. 1 2 3 4
Trb. 1 2
Bass
Eph.
Basses
Per.
Cymb. B. D.
cresc.
p cresc.
a2
ff

141
145
(one beat in a bar)
Picc.
Fl. 1 2
Ob.
E♭ Cl.
Cl. 1 2 3
B. Cl.
Bn. 1 2
Alto Sax.
Ten. Sax.
Bari. Sax.
fff
141
145
(one beat in a bar)
Cor. 1 2
Hn. 1 2 3 4
a2
Trb. 1 2
Bass
Eph.
Basses
Per.
Cymb. B. D.
fff

153
Picc.
Fl. 1 2
Ob.
E♭ Cl.
Cl. 1 2 3
B. Cl.
Bn. 1 2
Alto Sax.
Ten. Sax.
Bari. Sax.
153
Cor. 1 2
Hn. 1 2 3 4
Trb. 1 2
Bass
Eph.
Basses
Per.
Cymb.
B. D.

165
Picc.
Fl. 1 2
Ob.
E♭ Cl.
Cl. 1 2 3
dim.
B. Cl.
Bn. 1 2
Alto Sax.
Ten. Sax.
Bari. Sax.
p
165
Cor. 1 2
Hn. 1 2 3 4
Trb. 1 2
Bass
Eph.
Basses
Per.
Cymb. B. D.

177
two beats in a bar
Picc.
Fl. 1 2
Ob.
E♭ Cl.
Cl. 1 2 3
B. Cl.
Bn. 1 2
Alto Sax.
Ten. Sax.
Bari. Sax.
177
two beats in a bar
Cor. 1 2
Hn. 1 2 3 4
Trb. 1 2
Bass
Eph.
solo
Basses
tgl.
Per.
Cymb.
B. D.

189
Picc.
Fl. 1 2
Ob.
E♭ Cl.
Cl. 1 2 3
B. Cl.
Bn. 1 2
Alto Sax.
Ten. Sax.
Bari. Sax.
189
Cor. 1 2
Hn. 1 2 3 4
Trb. 1 2
Bass
Eph.
Basses
Per.
Cymb. B. D.
pp
(tutti)

201
solo
ppp
Picc.
Fl. 1 2
Ob.
E♭ Cl.
Cl. 1 2 3
B. Cl.
Bn. 1 2
ff
Alto Sax.
Ten. Sax.
Bari. Sax.
div.
con sord.
senza sord.
unis.
Cor. 1 2
Hn. 1 2 3 4
Trb. 1 2
Bass
Eph.
Basses
tutti
Per.
tamb.
Cymb. B. D.

www.ingramcontent.com/pod-product-compliance
Lightning Source LLC
Chambersburg PA
CBHW081153040426

42445CB00015B/1875